NETAJI THE UNSUNG HERO OF INDIA

ABHILASH CHAUBEY

Copyright © Abhilash Chaubey
All Rights Reserved.

This book has been published with all efforts taken to make the material error-free after the consent of the author. However, the author and the publisher do not assume and hereby disclaim any liability to any party for any loss, damage, or disruption caused by errors or omissions, whether such errors or omissions result from negligence, accident, or any other cause.

While every effort has been made to avoid any mistake or omission, this publication is being sold on the condition and understanding that neither the author nor the publishers or printers would be liable in any manner to any person by reason of any mistake or omission in this publication or for any action taken or omitted to be taken or advice rendered or accepted on the basis of this work. For any defect in printing or binding the publishers will be liable only to replace the defective copy by another copy of this work then available.

This Book is dedicated to all the soldiers of the Indian National Army, Netaji Subhash Chandra Bose and all those unsung and brave freedom fighter's of this great nation.
Jai Hind

Contents

Foreword

This is a book on Netaji Subhash Chandra Bose and his great INA, who did anything and everything to make our nation free.

In 1951 when Clement Atlee came to Indiahe was questioned by a journalist that why did they leave India as they had already won World War 2? His answer was simple Netaji and his INA.

What actually happened was that merciless Britisher's started a trial on the three top generals of INA for mutiny but the Royal Indian Navy sailors revolted and soon our whole country was engulfed in flames which compelled Britisher's to leave INA general's and our Nation

You will find more interesting truths in this book.

Preface

The aim of this book is to make our nation believe that we did not gain freedom from non-voilence and ahimsa, but with the help of great leaders such as Lal Gangadhar Tilak, Netaji Subhash Chandra Bose, Shaheed Bhagat Singh, Shaheed Udham Singh, Chandrashekhar Azad, Shaheed Sukhdev, Shaheed Rajguru and many more unsung hero's.

The aim is also to remind our present and upcoming generations about these great people. Jai Hind

Acknowledgements

I would like to thank our freedom fighters for their struggle, if they wished they would have happily lived a long life with luxurious lifestyle but they chose to live a difficult one only to make our nation free

Prologue

Netaji was born on 23rd January in 1897 in the city of Cuttack. His parents wanted him to become an ICS officer, he also became an ICS officer but destiny had other plans...

1
Birth of a Hero

The day was Saturday, 23rd January 1897 when Prabhati Bose, the wife of Janakinath Bose, gave birth to a healthy boy and they named him Subhash Chandra Bose. Since childhood he loved playing gully-danda. He used to listen the stories of Ram, Krishn, Maharana Pratap, Chatrapati Shivaji Maharaj and many other bravehearts from his grandmother.

By the age of four, he had good knowledge of folklores, the ramayan, the mahabharat and Indian History.

<u>Education</u>

At the age of 5, Subhash was admitted to the best school in town, Baptist Missionary School, Calicut. He scored highest marks in class 10 in Bengal and Central Province. He persuaded his class 12 from Ravenshaw Collegiate School in Cuttack, he got good marks in class 12th too. He got admission to the Presidency College in Calcutta. He was a good student and loved reading about great leaders such as Vladimir Lenin and Gandhi Ji. Many diseases such as Cholera and Small pox were spread in India like some wildfire. Subhash used to visit affected areas to help people. One such day he saw a mother crying besides her dead daughter, a son crying after his dead father, this changed him, from spiritual servitude to a social attitude. The British never provided Indians with medical facilities, which resulted with the deaths of more than 1.2 million Indian's. This made him think that all the facilities such as railway's, Medical facilities were made only for British people and not Indian's, In India.

2
The First Resistance

Subhash had a Professor in Presidency College by the name of Mr. E F Oaten, who was a big racist, he used to beat and punish Indian students for no reason, one such day he slapped subhash for no reason and subhash being a well-mannered student, did not do anything but the next day another student from his class was beaten so severely that he was admitted to a hospital, this enraged subhash and so, he and his friends beat Mr. O; which resulted in the eviction of Subhash from Presidency college.

After this his father, Jankinath Bose told him that it would be better for him to prepare for the ICS examinations, which is now known as UPSC examinations. So Subhash went to London for further studies, he completed the preparation only in four months, which took at least 2 and a half years at that time. At the time of results, Subhash had scored the third highest marks in the whole British Empire. After this in 1920 he was appointed as an ICS officer.

<u>The Non-Cooperation Movement</u>

The Non-Cooperation Movement was a political campaign launched in 1920, by Mahatma Gandhiji to have

Indian's revoke their cooperation from the British government, with the aim of including the British to grant self-governance. Gandhiji requested all Indian's to boycott foreign goods such as clothes, furniture and other foreign manufactured goods.

He also requested all Indian government officials to resign from their jobs, he requested all parents to take their children out of all government schools, colleges. The movement was one of Gandhi's first organized acts of large-scale satyagraha (civil disobedience). Gandhi's planning of the non-cooperation movement included persuading all Indians to withdraw their labour from any activity that "sustained the British government and also economy in India," including British industries and educational institutions. Through non-violent means, or Ahinsa, protesters would refuse to buy British goods, adopt the use of local handicrafts, and picket liquor shops. In addition to promoting "self-reliance" by spinning khadi, buying Indian-made goods only, and boycotting British goods, Gandhi's non-cooperation movement called for the restoration of the Khilafat (Khilafat movement) in Turkey and the end to untouchability. So after hearing this subhash immediately resigned from his ICS job, but destiny had other plans. A peaceful protest in Chauri-Chaura, a town in present day Uttar Pradesh, was fired upon by police; which led to death of more than 15 people. This enraged the crowd and they started beating police officers and soldiers, the policemen ran towards the police station and the crowd followed them. Panicking, policemen closed the doors of the station.

The crowd burned down the entire police station to ashes, which resulted in the death of 22 police men.After this Gandhiji took back the Non-cooperation movement and said that "This country is not prepared for

Independence. Children who previously attended government schools, colleges were not given admission to the schools, colleges, the govt officials were obviously not given their jobs back but Subhash joined the Indian National Congress in 1921 immediately after leaving his job in 1921.

3

Congress

Officially known as the Indian National Congress, it was founded in 1885. It was the first modern nationalist movement to emerge in the British Empire in Asia and Africa. Netaji joined the INC in 1921 immediately after resigning from his ICS job. He was a *karyakarta* under the great poet and nationalist Rabindranath Tagore, who understood Subhas's potential and immediately got him a place in the congress headquarters. Subhash was a great believer in the movement initiated by Gandhiji.

After Gandhiji took back the Non-Cooperation movement, Britisher's thought that if another non-cooperation movement would take place, they would be thrown out of the country. So to prevent this they made a commision led by Sir John Simon, commonly known as Simon commision. Its main objective was to prevent any mass movement in our country. All Nationalist parties including INC, Muslim league, the Gadar Party, The HSRA participated in protests against the commision. In a protest in Lahore, Lala Lajpat Rai was brutally killed in a lathi charge, ordered by Asst. Supritendent of police James A Scott. This led to the HSRA kill James Saunders, mistaking him to be scott. Gandhiji condemmed this act. Then in 1928 Lord Irwin gave a proposal to Gandhiji that they would happily make India a dominion status of the British Empire, Gandhiji agreed but even after 1 year no action was taken, wheareas Bhagat Singh, who was at that timwe in jail demandes *POORNA SWARAJ* meaning complete Independence, which was adopted by Jawaharlal Nehru in 1929 in Lahore congress session. On 23rd March 1931 Bhagat Singh, Sukhdev and Rajguru were cowardly hanged in Lahore jail, which resulted in mass protests and revolts.

In 1938 Subhash was sworn as the president of INC, Subhash being a supporter of violence to gain freedom, satarted becoming a problem for Gandhiji , who forcefully got subhash resign from the post of President in 1939.

4
The Great Escape

After his resignation from INC, Subhash founded a new party known as the Forward Bloc. It used violence to get Britisher's out of the country, however in 1940 the britisher's arrested him. He started a hunger strike till death and the only way to break it was that Britisher's leave subhash free from jail. They did everything to stop this Hunger strike but they could'nt so at the end they sent Subhash to his home in Kolkata. After this the Britisher's put Subhash under house arrest.

Netaji started a decoy plan, he declared that he was now a sanyasi and would not speak anything for a month. On the same night he escaped from his own house in a German Wanderer Sedan which was driven
by Netaji's nephew Sisir Kumar Bose.He was also dressed as a muslim insurance dealer who was going to Dhanbad. He then got into a train which was going from Dhanbad to Pesha

<u>HELP FROM KIRTI KISAN PARTY</u>

Netaji's plan was to escape from India and get help from the USSR. In this he would be helped by Chain Singh Chain from the KKP or the Kirti Kisan Party which was a communist party established in India. Bhagat Ram Talvar was a comrade in this party who had good ties with the Russian ambassador in Kabul. Hence Netaji escaped to Afghanistan were Bhagat Ram tried his best to convince the Russian ambassador but he couldn't. After which Netaji went to the German Ambassador and asked him if he could help him and the answer was yes.Netaji travelled to Italy and then to Germany

5

From Subhash to Netaji

After arriving in Germany Netaji finally met Adolf Hitler. Hitller used to have body doubles who were so similar looking to hitler that many times his military generals were also unable to differentiate between them, but Subhash easily identifeid the fake and real Hitler. On seeing this Adolf Hitler gave Subhash a name which is Netaji Subhash Chandra Bose. After a brief meeting it was decided that Netaji would travel from Germany to Japan in a U-boat (German submarine). After the meeting Netaji

started preparing for his journey, he would be accompained by Abid Hassan, his student since his days as the President is INC.

The journey was not easy, they had to semi circumnavigate the globe. Many times they encountered enemy patrol boats and destroyers. After coming on a decided point Netaji had to use a lifeboat to reach the Japanese sub. According to many eyewitnesses the sea waves were almost 16ft high then also Netaji assured them that he will do anything to let India get independence. Finally after this long journey Netaji landed in Indonesia. The Japanese Col. Hasegawa came to recieve him.

From Indonesia, Netaji took a flight to Tokyo to meet the then Prime Minister of Japanese Empire, **HIDEKI TOJO**, who believed that Asia belongs to Asian's not foreigner's. Both Tojo and Netai believed that India should be free and Tojo assured him that the Japanese Empire would be happy to assist Netaji gain his country's Independence.

6

INA Indian National Army

In 1942, Mohan Singh and Rash Bihari Bose founded an army comprising of British Indian Army men captured by the Japanese,, who were obviously Indians. Now Mohan Singh did not have good relation's with the Japanese, so the army was temporarily disbanded. When Netaji came back from Tokyo, he was made the leader of The Indian National Army on 4th July 1943.

<u>Accomplishments:</u>

On 23 October 1943, Azad Hind declared war against Britain and the United States. Its first formal commitment came with the opening of the Japanese offensive towards Manipur, code-named U-Go. In the initial plans for invasion of India, Field Marshall Terauschi had been reluctant to confer any responsibilities to the INA beyond espionage and propaganda. Netaji rejected this as the role of Fifth-columnists, and insisted that INA should contribute substantially in troops to form a distinct identity of an Indian-liberation army. He secured from Japanese army Chief of Staff, General Sugiyama, the agreement that INA

would rank as an allied army in the offensive. The advanced headquarters of Azad Hind was moved to Rangoon in anticipation of success. The INA's own strategy was to avoid set-piece battles, for which it lacked armament as well as manpower. Initially it sought to obtain arms and increase its ranks by inducing British-Indian soldiers to defect. The latter were expected to defect in large numbers. Col Prem Sahgal, once military secretary to Subhas Bose and later tried in the first Red Fort trials, explained the INA strategy to Peter Fay "although the war itself hung in balance and nobody was sure if the Japanese would win, initiating a popular revolution with grass-roots support within India would ensure that even if Japan ultimately lost the war, Britain would not be in a position to re-assert its colonial authority". It was planned that, once Japanese forces had broken through British defences at Imphal, the INA would cross the hills of North-East India into the Gangetic plain, where it would work as a guerrilla army.

Now when The United States started it's offensive against the Japanese, the supplies of the INA were affected; Medical supplies, food rations all of that was affected. After this the military and transport assistance was also pulled back. Now this led to a sudden defeat for INA in battles with the Chinese, US and the britisher's on the three sides of Burma(now Myanmar). After this the USAF(United States Air Forces) dropped two nuclear bombs in Hiroshima and Nagasaki on 6th and 9th of August in 1945 which made Japan surrender.

7
Mystery Behind the End

Singapore to Saigon

After Japanese surrender Netaji was requested by the Japanese army commander there, that he should talk to the Japanese front commander Fujiwara about what should he do next. So he took a flight from Singapore to Saigon. After a good and long meeting with Col Haswgawa and Gen Fujiwara, it was decided that he would go to Tokyo and meet Hideki Tojo, the then prime minister of Japan.

Saigon to Taihoku

After the meeting Netaji boarded a KI 21 bomber plane which was going to Tokyo via Taihoku. On 17 August 1945 Netaji's plane took off and landed at Taihoku. There was an overnight halt in Taihoku. Everybody had dinner, Rehman the person travelling with Netaji asked him if he too was feeling cold to which Netaji replied that "mujhe thand kam hi lagti hai". On the next day they boarded the plane at 5:05 AM and were ready for the take off.

The Plane Crash Theory

According to many people on the 18th of August 1945 the plane Netaji boarded the plane at 5 AM, it took off at 5:20 and just after 5 minutes it crashed and Netaji had third degree burns then he was taken to a nearby military hospital were he died. Netaji could not be taken to another place as there were no planes and the supplies required to presreve a body. Hence he was given a funeral and cremated in the hospital itself. His remains were placed at Renkoji Temple in Tokyo

8
Reality

——❦——

Reality

Reality was although a bit different, many people debate the accounts of 18th August 1945. Some points which are debatable are:

- Why did he take a Japanese plane when an INA plane with 12 seats was available.
- The soldiers who died in the plane never had cremation, military funeral.
- There are no such records of an aircrash, almost the death of 10 men on the airport, the local hospital.
- The eyevitnesses of this incident claim a different theory every time they are askrd.
- Why did an official farewell of Netaji take place, he was just going to Tojo for discussion on various topics.
- A journalist from New York Times had claimed that he saw Netaji in Manchuria on 21st of August 1945.
- Taiwan(then Taihoku) Government claims that no aircrash took place in the month of August in 1945

The USSR

As I said a journalist had claimed that he had seen Netaji in Manchuria. Our this section starts from manchuria as we see in the map, Manchuria had borders with south eastern parts of Soviet Union. Netaji had bluffed the whole world that he was no more but the reality is that he was in Soviet Union till 1968 where he had established a good freinship with Joseph Stalin and Nikita Krushchev. On one such occasion Ardhendu Sarkar, an engineer came to the Indian Embassy in Moscow. He met the ambassador and told him that a german pow of ww2 and his friend had seen and met Netaji. He said that a man who looked, talked like Netaji, visited the gulaag once and met him. He said that he had the riches of a Prime Minister, a Porche car, Gaurds and a very good income. Also a R&AW agent, on his death bed had told his friend that the Soviet minister they had met was none other than Netaji himself. Nikhil Chattopadhyay a tourist along with his wife had met Netaji in a Siberian town.

So by these eyewitnesses we get to know that Netaji had good relations with soviet premier's and there ministers. We also come to the conclusion that Netaji was in Soviet Union till 1968.

A Monk

After reading the above section all of us might have a question 'What happened after 1968?', then the answer is that he went to China in 1969 and there he became a monk and practiced buddhism. He had adopted buddhism so as to not be an odd one out and be a part of normal people. Another reason was that he also wanted to come back to India. So he did come to India in 1970 through Nepal. It is a rule that is still practised today that any Nepali citizen can enter India without passport or visa. Now another question poppes out that why did Netaji enter India in disguise? The answer is simple, allied powers wanted to treat him as a war criminal and give him harsh punishment although Russia and China were in good terms with Netaji but Britain and USA always wanted the same.

Gumnami Baba

After coming back to India Netaji did not want public attention due the the above reasons. So he started staying in a house in Alambh Bagh in Lucknow, which belonged to a Pandit. The then CM of Uttar Pradesh Ram Naresh Yadav frequently visited the baba or "bhagvanji" as people used to call him. This brought the public attention and hence bhagvanji shifted to Faizabad near Ayodhya in Uttar Pradesh. After which he spenned his rest of his life in secrecy and Gumnami.

Bibliography

1. What Happened to Netaji; Written By Anuj Dhar

2. An Indian Pilgrim; Written By Netaji Subhash Chandra Bose

3. The Indian Struggle; Written By Netaji Subhash Chandra Bose